The Ten Traits of High Performance Engineering Teams

AJAY LAKHANI

CONTENTS

Introduction

In the fast-paced, complex world of engineering, there is a select group of engineering teams that consistently achieve the extraordinary. Defying expectations, they surpass targets, pioneer innovations, and deliver results that exceed what was thought possible.

But what sets these high-performing teams apart?

In an environment of ever-accelerating technology, many engineering teams struggle to keep pace. Pressure mounts as the demand for speed and innovation increases. Complex challenges emerge that cannot be solved by individuals working alone. At the same time, attracting and retaining top engineering talent has become a pressing priority.

Now more than ever, there is a need to understand the inner workings of elite teams. What unique traits empower them to thrive amid growing complexity? How do they sustain excellence over the long term? What strategies enable them to rapidly innovate, pivot, and adapt?

The chapters ahead unravel the intricate tapestry of traits that collectively define and distinguish these teams. From fostering innovation, strategic alignment and cultivating collaborative cultures to confronting challenges with agility and adaptability, these traits go beyond technical prowess.

The goal of this playbook is to provide engineering teams and leaders with a practical guide to building and sustaining high performance. By exploring the core traits of successful teams, it aims to equip readers with strategies and insights to enhance team effectiveness.

KEY OBJECTIVES OF THIS PLAYBOOK

(1) Identify the fundamental characteristics that enable elite engineering team effectiveness.
(2) Learn proven strategies to cultivate key traits.
(3) Recognize common obstacles that arise when cultivating these traits and explore techniques to overcome them.

Whether you find yourself in a leadership role, aspire to excel as a team member, or are simply intrigued by the inner workings of exceptional teams, this exploration serves as a practical guide, revealing the keys to engineering success. Let's embark on a journey to understand what sets the best teams apart. The insights await in the pages ahead...

WHAT SETS HIGH-PERFORMING ENGINEERING TEAMS APART?

High-performing engineering teams are fueled by a distinct set of characteristics that enable them to operate at an elite level. These characteristics encompass a spectrum of qualities, ranging from technical prowess to effective collaboration and innovative problem-solving. By understanding the fundamental qualities that allow engineering teams to thrive in dynamic environments, we can uncover the building blocks for empowering teams to achieve their full potential.

This guide outlines the core characteristics that coalesce to drive exceptional performance. Let's explore the traits that set high-performing engineering teams on the path to success.

(1) *Technical Excellence*: High-performance engineering teams exhibit an unparalleled level of technical expertise. Team members possess a deep understanding of their respective domains, staying abreast of the latest advancements, methodologies, and tools relevant to their field.

(2) *Strategic Alignment*: These teams exhibit a unified vision and shared goals. This involves not only aligning on specific objectives and outcomes (Shared Goals) but also embracing a strategic vision that provides a guiding framework for the team's activities.

(3) *Effective Communication*: Whether conveying complex technical concepts, sharing project updates, or collaborating on solutions, effective communication promotes understanding and alignment among team

members, leading to streamlined workflows and successful project outcomes.

(4) *Continuously Learning*: Team members actively seek opportunities for professional development, stay curious about emerging technologies, and engage in knowledge-sharing activities.

(5) *Collaborative*: Effective teamwork and open communication foster an environment where diverse skills and perspectives converge.

(6) *Innovative Thinking*: These teams thrive on creativity and forward-thinking, constantly seeking novel approaches to problem-solving.

(7) *Agile and Adaptable*: These teams understand that flexibility is essential in a dynamic landscape, allowing them to pivot quickly in response to evolving requirements, unexpected challenges, or emerging opportunities.

(8) *Results-Driven*: They set clear goals, establish measurable objectives, and consistently deliver on expectations.

(9) *Resilience in the Face of Challenges*: Instead of viewing setbacks as failures, these teams treat them as opportunities for learning and improvement, adapting their strategies to navigate challenges effectively.

(10) *Passionate Engagement*: Team members in high-performance engineering teams are not just contributors; they are passionately engaged in their work.

While individual accountability, leadership support, trust, and diversity & inclusion are certainly important, the top ten traits drive high performance. Without excellence across these core areas, teams will struggle to realize their full potential, regardless of individual accountability, leadership style, interpersonal dynamics, or diversity factors.

Defining the characteristics of high-performing teams is an ongoing journey marked by a commitment to results, innovation, collaboration, and continuous growth. In the following chapters, we will explore strategies to cultivate these traits, guiding teams toward sustained high performance.

THE TEN TRAITS OF HIGH PERFORMING ENGINEERING TEAMS

.

1

TECHNICAL EXCELLENCE

In the fast-paced world of engineering, where new technologies and tools emerge at a staggering rate, technical excellence stands as a fundamental pillar of high performance. With the complexity of engineering challenges growing exponentially year-over-year, teams must continually expand their skills and knowledge to maintain a competitive edge. But how can organizations effectively adopt technical excellence amid this rapid change?

This chapter provides engineering leaders and professionals with strategies and insights to instill technical mastery within their teams. We will explore the critical components of technical excellence including fostering a growth mindset, pursuing breadth and depth of skills, implementing knowledge sharing, and leveraging leading-edge tools.

With the right strategies, engineering teams can unlock technical excellence to accelerate innovation cycles, reduce risks, and exceed customer expectations. This chapter equips engineering professionals at all levels with practical approaches to cultivate individual and collective technical mastery – empowering organizations to lead at the frontier of technology.

STRATEGIES FOR CULTIVATING TECHNICAL EXCELLENCE

Achieving sustainable technical excellence requires going beyond just acquiring skills. Teams need to take a thoughtful, strategic approach that fosters a culture of learning, collaboration, and innovation. Here are key strategies high-performing engineering teams leverage:

TECHNICAL EXCELLENCE

- Cultivate a Continuous Learning Culture
- Keep Updated on Technology Trends
- Implement Mentorship Programs
- Drive Innovation Initiatives
- Foster Cross-Functional Collaboration
- Document Best Practices
- Allocate Investment in Tools and Resources
- Conduct Research and Development
- Establish Actionable Feedback Loops
- Promote a Growth Mindset Culture

(1) *Cultivate a Continuous Learning Culture*: Foster ongoing technical growth through training, conferences, and knowledge sharing.
  - Dedicate time for ongoing education through "learn days" and technical talks.
  - Support conference/workshop attendance and sharing of key takeaways.
  - Maintain repository of educational resources.
(2) *Keep Updated on Technology Trends*: Stay current on emerging solutions by tracking trends, testing tools, and attending industry events.

- Assign ambassadors to track and share trends in their sub-domain.
- Test out new tools through proof-of-concept projects.
- Attend industry events to identify emerging solutions.

(3) *Implement Mentorship Programs*: Facilitate mentor-mentee relationships to provide tailored technical guidance.

- Facilitate formal and informal mentor-mentee relationships.
- Structure around technical domains to provide specialized guidance.
- Encourage reverse mentoring for fresh perspectives.

(4) *Drive Innovation Initiatives*: Spark creativity through hackathons and resources for experimenting with new methodologies.

- Host regular hackathons to spur creative thinking.
- Provide resources for experimenting with new methodologies.
- Recognize innovative contributions.

(5) *Foster Cross-Functional Collaboration*: Break down silos through interdisciplinary teams and knowledge exchange.

- Establish interdisciplinary project teams.
- Encourage knowledge sharing across domains.

(6) *Document Best Practices*: Capture technical expertise by maintaining accessible knowledge bases of best practices.

- Maintain knowledge base of internal best practices.
- Identify gaps through reviews and update docs.
- Make best practices easily accessible.

(7) *Invest in Tools and Resources:* Allocate budget to procure and provide training for essential tools.

- Survey team members on desired tools and allocate budget.
- Objectively evaluate options before purchasing.
- Appoint tool experts to provide ongoing training.

(8) *Conduct Research and Development:* Make time for experimentation with new techniques and showcase promising innovations.

- Structure 20% time for R&D efforts.

- Develop frameworks for experimenting before adoption.
- Showcase promising results in hackathons.

(9) *Establish Feedback Loops*: Gather regular input on skills, goals, and areas for improvement.

- Provide regular 1:1 feedback on skills and goals.
- Conduct anonymous surveys to identify improvements.
- Recognize top contributors publicly and privately.

(10) *Promote a Growth Mindset*: Destigmatize failure, take risks, and support continuous improvement.

- Destigmatize failure - treat setbacks as learning.
- Set ambitious goals requiring calculated risks.
- Support team members in identifying areas for growth.

By implementing these strategies, engineering teams can create an environment conducive to technical excellence, fostering continuous growth and innovation.

OVERCOMING CHALLENGES TO ACHIEVING TECHNICAL EXCELLENCE

Overcoming challenges to technical excellence in high-performance engineering teams requires a proactive and strategic approach. Here are key strategies to address common obstacles and ensure sustained technical excellence:

(1) *Resource Constraints:* Limited resources may hinder the team's ability to invest in essential tools, technologies, or talent.

- *Strategy*: Prioritize resource allocation based on critical technical needs. Advocate for additional resources, showcasing their impact on long-term performance. Explore external collaborations for supplementary expertise.

(2) *Resistance to Change*: Team members or stakeholders may resist adopting new technologies or methodologies.

- *Strategy*: Foster a culture that embraces change as a driver of improvement. Clearly communicate the benefits of proposed changes. Involve team members in decision-making to build ownership and acceptance of new approaches.

(3) *Skill Gaps and Training*: Skill gaps among team members can hinder the application of cutting-edge technologies.

- *Strategy*: Identify skill gaps through regular assessments. Implement targeted training programs to address specific technical deficiencies. Encourage continuous learning and pursuit of certifications.

(4) *Communication Breakdowns*: Ineffective communication channels can lead to misunderstandings and hinder technical collaboration.

- *Strategy*: Establish clear communication channels within the team. Leverage collaborative tools for information sharing. Conduct regular team meetings and check-ins to address concerns and maintain alignment.

(5) *Lack of Collaboration*: Siloed work environments can impede collaborative efforts among team members.

- *Strategy*: Foster a collaborative culture where cross-functional teams work seamlessly. Implement interdisciplinary projects to encourage collaboration between different engineering domains. Recognize and reward collaborative efforts.

(6) *Inadequate Feedback Mechanisms*: Lack of constructive feedback can hinder the identification and resolution of technical issues.

- *Strategy*: Establish regular feedback loops to assess technical performance. Encourage open and constructive feedback from peers and leaders. Implement 360-degree feedback mechanisms for diverse perspectives.

(7) *Insufficient Recognition*: Lack of acknowledgment for technical achievements may impact team morale.

- *Strategy*: Acknowledge and celebrate technical accomplishments within the team. Integrate recognition programs highlighting exemplary contributions to technical excellence. Ensure recognition extends beyond outcomes to include efforts and improvements.

(8) *Ineffective Project Management*: Poor project management practices can lead to inefficiencies and missed deadlines.

- *Strategy*: Implement robust project management practices to streamline workflows. Provide training in project management methodologies. Regularly assess and optimize project management processes based on team feedback.

(9) *Balancing Innovation and Stability*: Striking a balance between innovation and maintaining system stability can be challenging.

- *Strategy*: Create a structured innovation framework that balances risk-taking with stability. Designate specific projects or timeframes for exploring innovative solutions. Ensure stability while fostering a culture of innovation.

(10) *Lack of Cross-Functional Exposure*: Limited exposure to different engineering disciplines may narrow team members' perspectives.

- *Strategy*: Facilitate opportunities for cross-functional exposure. Encourage rotations or cross-functional projects to broaden skill sets. Promote a holistic understanding of the organization's technical landscape.

By addressing these challenges with the outlined strategies, high-performance engineering teams can fortify their commitment to technical excellence and navigate the complexities of the dynamic engineering landscape successfully.

2

STRATEGIC ALIGNMENT

In today's complex business landscapes, having a powerful strategic vision is indispensable for engineering teams striving for high performance. Beyond mastering immediate technical tasks, truly exceptional teams align on shared objectives that tie directly to organizational goals. This strategic orientation comes to life through a unified vision that provides direction and purpose. When team members grasp how their work ladders up to strategic impact, it unlocks higher levels of motivation, collaboration, and innovation.

But how can leaders effectively cultivate strategic alignment within their organizations? This chapter provides engineering managers and professionals with insights on fostering a strategically-oriented culture. With the right approaches, engineering teams can become powerfully aligned to company strategy, guiding their efforts with shared purpose. This clarity of direction empowers skilled teams to maximize their collaboration, innovation, and value creation. By unpacking the facets of strategic orientation, this chapter equips engineering leaders to build high-performing teams that execute strategic objectives with excellence.

STRATEGIES FOR STRATEGIC ALIGNMENT

Instilling a shared sense of purpose and common values within engineering teams requires thoughtful leadership and inclusion of all members. Here are key strategies and techniques leaders can leverage:

STRATEGIC ALIGNMENT

- Define a Compelling Strategic Vision
- Collaboratively Set Objectives
- Establish Core Values:
- Consistently Communicate Purpose
- Lead by Example
- Break Down Silos
- Recognize Values in Action
- Gather Continuous Feedback
- Invest in Team Building
- Embrace Diversity and Inclusion

(1) *Define a Compelling Strategic Vision*: Develop a unifying vision that aligns with organizational goals.
   - Conduct annual offsite with leadership to define 3-year vision.
   - Align vision to company's mission, values, and growth objectives.

- Make the vision forward-looking, inspiring, and attainable by the team.

(2) *Collaboratively Set Objectives*: Include all team members in the goal-setting process to build a sense of ownership.

- Gather input from all team members during annual planning workshop.
- Set quarterly OKRs based on team member submissions.
- Re-evaluate OKRs each quarter and adjust as needed.

(3) *Establish Core Values*: Lead an inclusive process to define core values, gathering input from all team members.

- Facilitate collaborative brainstorming session to define values.
- Distill input into top 3-5 values that resonate most.
- Integrate values into team charter displayed in office.

(4) *Consistently Communicate Purpose*: Reference the team's purpose and values consistently in meetings and communications.

- Start all major meetings recapping vision, objectives, values.
- Reference values when evaluating options and making decisions.
- Share stories monthly of values embodied in projects.

(5) *Lead by Example*: Leaders should exemplify the behaviors encapsulated in the team's values.

- Showcase leaders who consistently demonstrate the team's values in their decisions and conduct.
- Hold leaders accountable for upholding and promoting the team's values.
- Incorporate values into leadership feedback process.

(6) *Break Down Silos*: Actively encourage interdisciplinary collaboration and knowledge sharing.

- Structure interdisciplinary project teams that rotate members
- Host brown bag series with speakers from different departments

- Recognize cross-department collaboration with awards.

(7) *Recognize Values in Action*: Recognize and celebrate behaviors that reflect the core values through awards or acknowledgment.

- Give "Values in Action" shout-outs in meetings.
- Feature story monthly of project reflecting values.
- Incorporate values embodiment into performance reviews.

(8) *Gather Continuous Feedback*: Create open channels for team members to provide input on how well values are embodied.

- Conduct brief pulse survey on values quarterly.
- Discuss areas of misalignment in team retrospectives
- Solicit anonymous input on aligning behaviors to values.

(9) *Invest in Team Building*: Organize activities focused on building a shared team identity and purpose.

- Hold biannual offsite for team building activities.
- Organize monthly team lunches and social events.
- Bring in facilitator for workshops on trust and communication.

(10) *Embrace Diversity and Inclusion*: Integrate diversity and inclusion within the team's core values.

- Provide unconscious bias training for all team members.
- Emphasize the benefits of diverse perspectives in problem-solving and innovation.
- Recruit team members with diverse backgrounds and perspectives.

By dedicatedly implementing these strategies, leaders empower high-performance engineering teams to thrive, unite, and excel. Purpose and principles serve as the guiding light, illuminating the path to sustained high performance.

OVERCOMING CHALLENGES TO
STRATEGIC ALIGNMENT

While establishing a shared purpose and values is instrumental for high-performance engineering teams, challenges may emerge that require strategic solutions. Addressing these challenges head-on ensures that the team remains aligned and focused on a collective vision. Here are strategies to overcome common challenges associated with cultivating a shared purpose and values:

(1) *Ambiguous Vision and Goals*: Lack of a clear vision or well-defined goals can lead to confusion and misalignment.
   - *Strategy*: Clearly articulate an inspiring vision for the team and collaboratively set specific, measurable, and achievable objectives. Ensure that every team member understands and aligns with the overarching purpose.
(2) *Resistance to Change*: Team members may resist changes in processes, methodologies, or strategic direction.
   - *Strategy*: Foster a culture that embraces change as an opportunity for improvement. Communicate the benefits of proposed changes transparently and involve team members in decision-making to enhance acceptance and ownership.
(3) *Lack of Clarity*: Ambiguity or lack of clarity regarding the shared purpose and values can lead to confusion and misinterpretation.
   - *Strategy*: Clearly define and communicate the shared purpose and values using accessible language. Provide concrete examples of how these principles manifest in daily activities to enhance understanding.
(4) *Inconsistent Leadership Alignment*: Inconsistency in leadership alignment with the shared purpose can create confusion among team members.
   - *Strategy*: Ensure that leadership is uniformly committed to and demonstrates alignment with the established

purpose and values. Provide leadership training to reinforce the importance of consistent messaging.

(5) *Failure to Integrate Values into Processes*: If values are not integrated into daily processes and decision-making, they may remain superficial and fail to guide behavior.

- *Strategy*: Infuse values into all aspects of team operations. This includes hiring processes, project planning, and performance evaluations. Aligning values with tangible actions reinforces their significance.

(6) *Cultural Disconnect*: Team members from diverse cultural backgrounds may interpret shared values differently, leading to a cultural disconnect.

- *Strategy*: Promote inclusivity and open discussions about cultural interpretations of values. Create a space where team members can share their perspectives, fostering a more nuanced understanding of the shared purpose.

(7) *Insufficient Communication*: Inadequate communication about the ongoing relevance and application of shared values may result in team members losing sight of their significance.

- *Strategy*: Establish regular communication channels dedicated to reinforcing the team's shared purpose and values. Celebrate instances where values are exemplified, keeping them at the forefront of team consciousness.

(8) *Mismatch Between Individual and Team Values*: Team members may feel a misalignment between their personal values and those emphasized by the team.

- *Strategy*: Encourage open dialogue about individual values and their alignment with the team's values. Where possible, find common ground or identify ways to leverage diverse values for collective benefit.

(9) *Inadequate Recognition*: Lack of recognition for individuals who exemplify the team's values may diminish the importance of those values.

- *Strategy*: Establish a robust recognition system that acknowledges and celebrates instances where team members embody shared values. Recognition reinforces the importance of collective adherence.

(10) *Overemphasis on Short-Term Goals*: Pressures to meet immediate project goals may shift focus away from the long-term vision and shared purpose.

- *Strategy*: Balance short-term objectives with a continuous reinforcement of the team's shared purpose. Communicate how achieving short-term goals contributes to the overarching vision.

By systematically addressing these top 10 challenges with the outlined strategies, high-performance engineering teams can strengthen their commitment to strategic alignment and navigate the complexities of their dynamic landscape effectively.

3

EFFECTIVE COMMUNICATION

Clear and open communication stands as a cornerstone of effective collaboration in engineering teams. With complex projects involving multiple stakeholders, miscommunications can swiftly derail progress. But communication mastery enables seamless coordination, context sharing, and transparent decision-making.

This chapter provides engineering leaders and professionals with strategies to instill a culture of effective communication. We will explore techniques for aligning on terminology, managing meetings productively, documenting work transparently and giving constructive feedback.

With the right communication principles, engineering teams can minimize misunderstandings, accelerate projects, and enhance team cohesion. By unpacking the elements of frequent, clear, and considerate communication, this chapter empowers engineering organizations to execute collaboratively at the highest levels.

STRATEGIES FOR EFFECTIVE COMMUNICATION

Clear and open communication is the cornerstone of success for high-performance engineering teams. To cultivate a communicative environment that enhances collaboration and efficiency, consider the following key strategies:

(1) *Ensure Clear Communication Channels*: Set up accessible platforms for collaboration, chatting, documentation and updates.
   - Set up project management platform like Jira for task tracking.
   - Use Slack/Teams for real-time messaging and questions.
   - Email weekly summaries of key updates and next steps

- Document requirements, notes, and specs on team's SharePoint site.

(2) *Establish Communication Protocols*: Establish clear guidelines for utilizing different communication channels appropriately.

- Email for formal notices, status reports, and documents
- Slack for quick questions and updates
- Specify 24 hr. email response time.
- Set conventions for version control and naming files.

(3) *Conduct Regular Team Meetings*: Conduct recurring syncs to align on status, goals and address concerns.

- Weekly 30 min status meeting to discuss projects and blockers.
- Daily 15 min stand-up for quick progress updates
- Monthly 1 hr. retrospective to improve processes.

(4) *Structure Documentation*: Maintain thorough documentation of requirements, decisions, and specifications.

- Log all design decisions and rationale in knowledge base.
- Annotate diagrams with technical explanations.
- Use templates for meeting notes, status reports, and presentations.

(5) *Practice Active Listening*: Give full attention to thoroughly understand context and meaning.

- Make eye contact and give full attention in meetings.
- Paraphrase what was said to confirm understanding.
- Ask clarifying questions rather than make assumptions.

(6) *Implement Feedback Loops*: Gather regular input to drive continuous improvement.

- Gather feedback every 2 weeks during sprint demos.
- Conduct anonymous surveys quarterly to identify improvements.
- Share constructive feedback 1-on-1 in regular check-ins.

(7) *Utilize Visual Communication Tools*: Leverage diagrams, charts, and visuals to convey complex concepts clearly.

- Explain architectures with system diagrams.
- Annotate screenshots to illustrate UI behaviour.
- Create flowcharts and entity relationship diagrams to map processes.

(8) *Foster Cross-Functional Collaboration*: Facilitate interactions between different disciplines for diverse perspectives.

- Rotate members across sub-teams each quarter.
- Assign mentors from other disciplines.
- Host brown bag talks on different engineering topics.

(9) *Make Decision-Making Transparent*: Clearly explain rationale behind choices to build trust.

- Document key decisions in meeting notes with rationale
- Recap decisions at the start of each new meeting
- Solicit input from team before finalizing major decisions.

(10) *Provide Regular Status Updates*: Share frequent progress to maintain alignment on blockers.

- Start stand-ups with 3 key updates from each member.
- Share detailed progress reports before each sprint demo.
- Update Jira tickets frequently to maintain transparency.

By focusing on these key strategies, engineering teams can fortify their communication framework, fostering an environment where information flows seamlessly, ideas flourish, and collaboration thrives.

OVERCOMING CHALLENGES TO EFFECTIVE COMMUNICATION

While effective communication is essential for the success of high-performance engineering teams, various challenges may impede its seamless implementation. Addressing these challenges proactively is crucial to ensure that communication remains a catalyst for collaboration rather than a barrier. Here are strategies to overcome common challenges associated with cultivating effective communication in high-performance engineering teams:

(1) *Communication Silos*: Silos within the team can hinder the free flow of information, leading to incomplete understanding and misalignment.
   - *Strategy*: Implement cross-functional collaboration initiatives, encourage interdisciplinary interactions, and utilize project management tools that facilitate transparent communication across all team members.

(2) *Language Barriers*: In multicultural teams, language differences may result in misunderstandings and misinterpretations.
   - *Strategy*: Promote language proficiency development, provide language training if necessary, and encourage team members to express themselves in the language they are most comfortable with to enhance clarity.

(3) *Time Zone Differences*: Teams distributed across different time zones may face challenges in coordinating real-time communication.
   - *Strategy*: Establish overlapping working hours, utilize asynchronous communication tools, and clearly define expectations regarding response times to accommodate and respect time zone differences.

(4) *Overreliance on Written Communication*: Depending solely on written communication may lead to information overload and hinder nuanced understanding.
   - *Strategy*: Integrate verbal communication methods, such as regular video calls or virtual meetings, to complement written communication. This provides opportunities for real-time clarification and fosters a sense of connection.

(5) *Information Overload*: Excessive information can overwhelm team members, leading to important details being overlooked.

- *Strategy*: Streamline communication by prioritizing essential information, utilizing concise formats, and establishing clear channels for critical updates. This ensures that key messages are not lost amid an overload of data.

(6) *Lack of Communication Skills*: Team members may lack effective communication skills, resulting in unclear messages and misinterpretations.

- *Strategy*: Provide regular training on communication skills, including both verbal and written communication. Encourage the development of interpersonal skills to enhance the effectiveness of team interactions.

(7) *Resistance to New Communication Tools*: Resistance to adopting new communication tools may impede the integration of efficient and collaborative platforms.

- *Strategy*: Offer comprehensive training on new tools, highlight the benefits of adoption, and address concerns proactively. Create a culture that values and embraces the use of technology for streamlined communication.

(8) *Inadequate Feedback Culture*: A lack of constructive feedback mechanisms can hinder improvement in communication practices.

- *Strategy*: Establish a feedback-rich environment, encourage team members to provide feedback on communication processes, and conduct regular evaluations to identify areas for enhancement.

(9) *Failure to Document Important Information*: Not documenting crucial decisions or information can result in knowledge gaps and misunderstandings.

- *Strategy*: Implement structured documentation practices, emphasizing the importance of recording key decisions, project updates, and relevant discussions. Ensure that documentation is easily accessible to all team members.

(10) *Insufficient Time for Communication*: High workloads and
tight schedules may limit the time available for effective
communication.

- *Strategy*: Prioritize communication as a critical aspect of
project success. Allocate dedicated time for team
meetings, updates, and discussions to ensure that
communication is not overlooked amidst competing
priorities.

By actively addressing these challenges, high-performance
engineering teams can fortify their communication practices,
ensuring that information is shared effectively,
misunderstandings are minimized, and the team operates
cohesively towards achieving their objectives. Effective
communication becomes a dynamic force that propels the
team forward in the pursuit of engineering excellence.

4

CONTINUOSLY LEARNING

In the fast-paced world of technology, continuous learning is imperative for engineering teams striving for high performance. With rapid innovation cycles, the skills and knowledge that make teams successful today may quickly become obsolete tomorrow. But organizations that instill a culture of continuous learning position themselves for the future.

A Continuous Learning Culture is more than a strategy; it's a mindset that fosters a relentless commitment to learning, adaptation, and perpetual enhancement. It recognizes that the journey to engineering excellence is a continuous cycle of exploration, learning from experiences, and leveraging newfound insights to elevate both individual capabilities and team performance. This chapter provides engineering leaders and professionals with strategies to foster an environment of ongoing learning and growth. We will explore approaches including mentorship programs, job rotation schemes, incentivized certifications, hackathons, and real-time feedback.

With the right learning culture, engineering teams can rapidly adopt new competencies, leverage innovations, and expand their capabilities. By unpacking the elements of individual and collective continuous skill enhancement, this chapter empowers engineering organizations to unlock their greatest potential for the challenges ahead.

STRATEGIES FOR CULTIVATING A CONTINUOUS LEARNING CULTURE

Cultivating such a culture requires intentional strategies that foster an environment where every team member is empowered to contribute to their professional development and the collective growth of the team. Here are strategies to instill and nurture a Continuous Learning Culture within your high-performance engineering team:

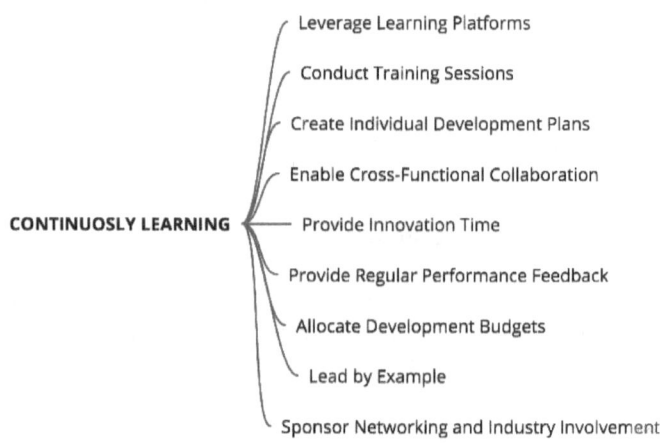

(1) *Leverage Learning Platforms*: Provide subscriptions to online learning platforms like Pluralsight that offer extensive technical course libraries for self-driven learning.

- Provide $500 annual subscriptions to platforms like Pluralsight, Udemy, O'Reilly, etc. Allow employees to choose platforms based on course libraries.
- Encourage use of platforms for self-guided learning during Friday "Learning Days". Have employees share key lessons.

(2) *Conduct Training Sessions*: Schedule workshops and upskilling sessions focused on high priority skills and project-specific needs.

- Schedule bi-weekly Lunch & Learns led by team members to share expertise.
- Conduct quarterly 2–3-day intensive workshops on priority skills like React, Cloud Certifications, Algorithms, etc.

(3) *Create Individual Development Plans*: Collaborate to outline personalized learning goals, timelines, and metrics tailored to close skill gaps.

- Set annual IDP meetings for managers and employees to collaborate on skills to develop, metrics, and timelines tailored to project needs.
- Revisit IDPs quarterly to adjust goals based on shifting priorities. Track progress through metrics like courses completed.

(4) *Enable Cross-Functional Collaboration*: Facilitate collaboration across disciplines through rotations, shadowing, and cross-functional workshops.

- Implement 6-month rotations across teams to gain exposure to different technologies and approaches.
- Structure monthly cross-team workshops for collaborative problem solving.

(5) *Develop Mentorship Programs*: Establish initiatives that pair junior and senior team members for guidance and knowledge sharing.

- Kick off a formal mentorship program pairing junior and senior engineers. Outline program structure, goals and duration.
- Encourage organic informal mentorships through networking events and activity-based meetups.

(6) *Provide Innovation Time*: Institute unstructured time for experimentation, passion projects, and self-directed learning.

- Every Friday, dedicate 2 hours for employees to work on passion projects, R&D, or learning. Share innovations in Demo Day events.

- Allow employees to use 10% of their time for self-directed innovation initiatives.

(7) *Regular Performance Feedback*: Conduct consistent reviews focused on individual development, strengths, improvements and goals.

- Hold quarterly 1-on-1s between managers and direct reports focused on goals, development areas, and career aspirations.
- Conduct weekly informal check-ins on current projects, challenges, and short-term wins.
- Seek feedback from stakeholders on performance and areas for improvement.

(8) *Individual Development Budgets*: Provide personalized budgets for pursuing learning through conferences, courses, and materials.

- Provide $1000 annual individual learning stipend that can cover conferences, online courses, workshops, books/materials.
- Allow roll-over of unused budget each year to encourage continual investment in growth.
- Require Development Plans showing how budget will be used to address skills gaps.

(9) *Lead by Example*: Managers should visibly model continuous learning behaviors and share their own development.

- Managers share lessons from books/courses during team meetings to demonstrate commitment to learning.
- Leaders voluntarily participate in ride-alongs, mentorships and peer exchanges to continue developing.
- Managers incorporate mentorship and learning goals into their own development plans.

(10) *Sponsor Networking and Industry Involvement*: Support participation in industry events, technical consortiums, conferences and professional networking.

- Sponsor attendance at leading industry conferences like AWS re:Invent. Require sharing of top insights.

- Enable participation in local meetup groups, hackathons, and technical consortiums.
- Volunteer as speakers at industry conferences, demonstrate thought leadership.

By weaving these strategies into the fabric of your high-performance engineering team, you can cultivate a culture of Continuous Learning that not only adjusts to the evolving demands of the industry but thrives on the collective pursuit of excellence and ongoing improvement.

OVERCOMING CHALLENGES TO FOSTERING A CULTURE OF CONTINUOUS LEARNING

While striving to instill a Continuous Learning Culture within high-performance engineering teams, certain challenges may emerge, requiring strategic approaches for effective resolution. Addressing these challenges head-on is essential to ensure that the team can collectively overcome obstacles and maintain an environment conducive to continuous learning and improvement. Here are strategies to overcome common challenges associated with cultivating a Continuous Learning Culture:

(1) *Communication Silos*: Silos within the team can hinder the free flow of information, leading to incomplete understanding and misalignment.
   - *Strategy*: Implement cross-functional collaboration initiatives, encourage interdisciplinary interactions, and utilize project management tools that facilitate transparent communication across all team members.
(2) *Language Barriers*: In multicultural teams, language differences may result in misunderstandings and misinterpretations.
   - *Strategy*: Promote language proficiency development, provide language training if necessary, and encourage

team members to express themselves in the language they are most comfortable with to enhance clarity.

(3) *Time Zone Differences*: Teams distributed across different time zones may face challenges in coordinating real-time communication.

- *Strategy*: Establish overlapping working hours, utilize asynchronous communication tools, and clearly define expectations regarding response times to accommodate and respect time zone differences.

(4) *Overreliance on Written Communication*: Depending solely on written communication may lead to information overload and hinder nuanced understanding.

- *Strategy*: Integrate verbal communication methods, such as regular video calls or virtual meetings, to complement written communication. This provides opportunities for real-time clarification and fosters a sense of connection.

(5) *Information Overload*: Excessive information can overwhelm team members, leading to important details being overlooked.

- *Strategy*: Streamline communication by prioritizing essential information, utilizing concise formats, and establishing clear channels for critical updates. This ensures that key messages are not lost amid an overload of data.

(6) *Lack of Communication Skills*: Team members may lack effective communication skills, resulting in unclear messages and misinterpretations.

- *Strategy*: Provide regular training on communication skills, including both verbal and written communication. Encourage the development of interpersonal skills to enhance the effectiveness of team interactions.

(7) *Resistance to New Communication Tools*: Resistance to adopting new communication tools may impede the integration of efficient and collaborative platforms.

- *Strategy*: Offer comprehensive training on new tools, highlight the benefits of adoption, and address concerns proactively. Create a culture that values and embraces the use of technology for streamlined communication.

(8) *Inadequate Feedback Culture*: A lack of constructive feedback mechanisms can hinder improvement in communication practices.

- *Strategy*: Establish a feedback-rich environment, encourage team members to provide feedback on communication processes, and conduct regular evaluations to identify areas for enhancement.

(9) *Failure to Document Important Information*: Not documenting crucial decisions or information can result in knowledge gaps and misunderstandings.

- *Strategy*: Implement structured documentation practices, emphasizing the importance of recording key decisions, project updates, and relevant discussions. Ensure that documentation is easily accessible to all team members.

(10) *Insufficient Time for Communication*: High workloads and tight schedules may limit the time available for effective communication.

- *Strategy*: Prioritize communication as a critical aspect of project success. Allocate dedicated time for team meetings, updates, and discussions to ensure that communication is not overlooked amidst competing priorities.

By proactively addressing these challenges, high-performance engineering teams can create a resilient Continuous Learning Culture, ensuring that every obstacle becomes an opportunity for learning and improvement.

5

COLLABORATIVE

In the dynamic realm of high-performance engineering, collaboration stands as the cornerstone of innovation, efficiency, and overall team success. As engineering challenges grow in complexity, the need for collective synergy becomes paramount. High-performing teams are not merely a collection of individual talents; they are a cohesive unit where diverse minds converge to tackle challenges with shared objectives.

Chapter 5 delves into the profound significance of fostering a collaborative culture within engineering teams, exploring how collaboration becomes the catalyst for breaking down silos, enhancing interdisciplinary interactions, and instilling a shared sense of ownership. This chapter unravels the core principles and strategic approaches that underpin a collaborative culture, illuminating its pivotal role in navigating the intricacies of modern projects.

As we journey through the strategies outlined in this chapter, it becomes evident that fostering collaboration is more than a methodology – it's a mindset that elevates individual contributions to a collective brilliance. From defining a common purpose to celebrating team achievements, from encouraging cross-functional collaboration to providing collaborative tools and technologies, each strategy plays a vital role in shaping a collaborative culture that propels engineering teams toward sustained success.

STRATEGIES FOR CULTIVATING A COLLABORATIVE CULTURE

Cultivating a collaborative culture within a high-performance engineering team involves intentional strategies that promote teamwork, open communication, and shared goals. Here are some effective strategies for fostering a collaborative culture:

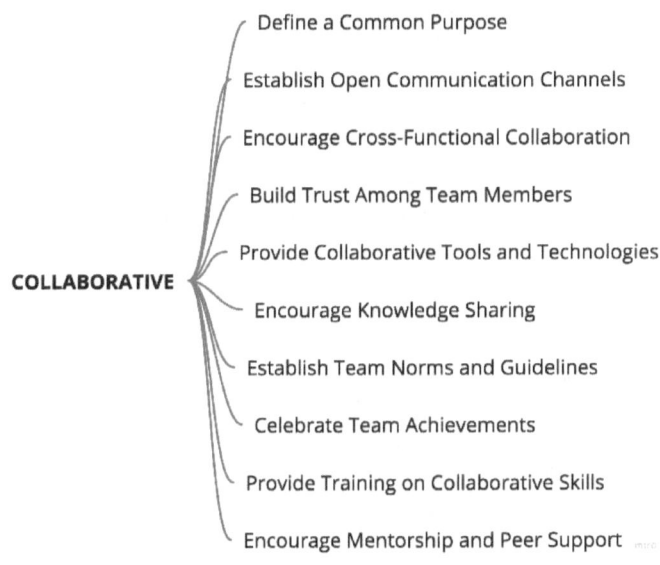

COLLABORATIVE

- Define a Common Purpose
- Establish Open Communication Channels
- Encourage Cross-Functional Collaboration
- Build Trust Among Team Members
- Provide Collaborative Tools and Technologies
- Encourage Knowledge Sharing
- Establish Team Norms and Guidelines
- Celebrate Team Achievements
- Provide Training on Collaborative Skills
- Encourage Mentorship and Peer Support

(1) *Define a Common Purpose*: Craft a shared mission statement aligning the team's vision and goals.
- Conduct a visioning exercise where members imagine the ideal future team culture.
- Draft a mission statement and review it during an all-hands meeting to gather feedback.
- Use the mission statement as a guidepost for decision-making and resolving conflicts.

(2) *Establish Open Communication Channels*: Implement platforms to enable open team discussions and real-time information sharing.

- Implement daily stand-up meetings for quick updates.
- Schedule regular 1-on-1s for deeper discussions.
- Use Slack channels focused on different projects, technologies, etc.

(3) *Encourage Cross-Functional Collaboration*: Promote collaborative projects across disciplines to spur innovation.

- Organize hackathons focused on a shared goal like improving site performance.
- Assign mixed skill teams to develop new feature mockups.
- Structure coffee meetings between departments.

(4) *Build Trust Among Team Members*: Foster psychological safety for honest interactions and accountability.

- Host a team retreat with trust-building activities like escape rooms.
- Encourage weekly peer feedback sessions to recognize achievements.
- Create psychological safety for expressing opinions and concerns.

(5) *Provide Collaborative Tools and Technologies*: Supply tools for remote collaboration, brainstorming, and seamless workflow.

- Use Miro for remote brainstorming sessions.
- Implement GitHub for collaborative coding and code reviews.
- Test VR meeting software like Gather for more immersive interactions.

(6) *Encourage Knowledge Sharing*: Create channels for team members to exchange insights and best practices.

- Send out a weekly digest of lessons learned and best practices.
- Add searchable tags to project documentation.

- Record tech talks and make available on a shared drive.

(7) *Establish Team Norms and Guidelines:* Document clear protocols and etiquette for teamwork and decision-making.

- Document procedures for sprint planning, standups, retrospectives.
- Outline communication best practices like active listening.
- Define escalation processes for conflict resolution.

(8) *Celebrate Team Achievements:* Highlight milestones and wins through public recognition.

- Give shoutouts for wins during standup meetings.
- Organize quarterly events to highlight major milestones.
- Create a visible scoreboard tracking team goals.

(9) *Provide Training on Collaborative Skills:* Teach techniques for better communication, conflict resolution, and collaboration.

- Host a workshop on effective stakeholder communication.
- Bring in an expert to teach negotiation and conflict resolution tactics.
- Distribute resources on techniques like active listening.

(10) *Encourage Mentorship and Peer Support:* Facilitate guidance and growth through mentor/mentee and peer learning.

- Match senior and junior members for guidance and growth.
- Structure peer exchanges to learn from diverse experiences.
- Foster an ask-anything culture without judgment.

By implementing these strategies, engineering teams can create a collaborative culture that not only enhances productivity but also fosters innovation and resilience in the face of complex challenges. A collaborative culture is not just a means to an end but a vital element that propels high-performance engineering teams toward sustained success.

OVERCOMING CHALLENGES TO BUILDING A COLLABORATIVE CULTURE

Cultivating a collaborative culture within high-performance engineering teams is a dynamic process that brings numerous benefits, but it's not without its challenges. Addressing these challenges head-on is essential to ensure that the team can collectively overcome obstacles and maintain an environment conducive to effective collaboration.

(1) *Resistance to Change*: Some team members may resist adopting new collaborative practices or changes to existing workflows.
- *Strategy*: Communicate the benefits of collaborative culture clearly, emphasizing personal and collective growth. Involve the team in decision-making processes to increase buy-in and facilitate a smoother transition. Showcase success stories where collaboration led to positive outcomes.

(2) *Siloed Work Environments*: Silos within the team can hinder cross-functional collaboration, leading to incomplete understanding and misalignment.
- *Strategy*: Implement cross-functional collaboration initiatives, encourage interdisciplinary interactions, and utilize project management tools that facilitate transparent communication across all team members. Foster a culture that values and promotes collaboration across different functional areas.

(3) *Lack of Effective Communication*: Ineffective communication channels can result in misunderstandings and hinder the free flow of information.
- *Strategy*: Establish clear communication channels, utilize collaborative tools for real-time updates, and conduct regular training on effective communication.

Implement guidelines for communication etiquette to streamline information exchange.

(4) *Team Dynamics and Trust Issues*: Building trust among team members can be challenging, especially in virtual or distributed team setups.

- *Strategy*: Organize team-building activities, encourage open feedback sessions, and establish a culture of accountability. Foster an environment where team members feel comfortable sharing ideas and collaborating without fear of judgment.

(5) *Balancing Individual and Team Goals*: Individual goals may sometimes conflict with team objectives, leading to challenges in collaboration.

- *Strategy*: Align individual and team goals through clear communication and goal-setting sessions. Emphasize the collective impact of achieving team objectives on individual growth and success.

(6) *Lack of Inclusivity*: Some team members may feel excluded, leading to a breakdown in collaboration.

- *Strategy*: Promote inclusivity through team-wide initiatives, encourage diverse perspectives, and provide platforms for all team members to contribute. Implement guidelines that ensure everyone's voice is heard and valued.

(7) *Time Zone and Location Differences*: Teams distributed across different time zones may face challenges in coordinating real-time collaboration.

- *Strategy*: Establish overlapping working hours, utilize asynchronous communication tools, and clearly define expectations regarding response times. Implement flexible scheduling options to accommodate global team dynamics.

(8) *Technological Barriers*: Inadequate or unfamiliar collaborative tools can hinder effective virtual teamwork.

- *Strategy*: Invest in user-friendly collaborative technologies, provide comprehensive training on their usage, and encourage ongoing exploration of new tools that enhance virtual collaboration.

(9) *Leadership Support and Modeling*: Lack of leadership support or modeling collaborative behavior can impact team culture.

- *Strategy*: Actively involve leadership in collaborative initiatives, emphasize the importance of collaboration in achieving organizational goals, and encourage leaders to model collaborative behaviors. Provide training for leadership on fostering a collaborative culture.

(10) *Measuring and Recognizing Collaboration*: It may be challenging to measure and recognize the collaborative efforts of team members.

- *Strategy*: Implement performance metrics that reflect collaborative contributions, recognize and celebrate collaborative achievements, and tie collaboration to performance evaluations. Showcase examples where collaboration led to project success.

By addressing these challenges proactively and implementing tailored strategies, high-performance engineering teams can create a collaborative culture that not only overcomes obstacles but also thrives in the face of complex engineering projects. It's a continuous process of adaptation and improvement, ensuring that the collaborative culture remains a driving force behind the team's success.

6

INNOVATIVE THINKING

Innovation stands at the heart of problem-solving and progress for engineering teams. Beyond just technical expertise, truly high-performing teams think creatively to generate novel solutions and push boundaries. But how can leaders spark innovative thinking?

This chapter provides engineering managers and professionals with strategies to build a culture of innovation by embracing creativity, prototyping new ideas, allowing failure on the path to success, and collaborating across disciplines.

With the right environment, teams can amplify innovative thinking to accelerate development cycles, reduce project risks, and deliver unprecedented value. By exploring tactics to spur imagination, constructively debate ideas, and experiment with solutions, this chapter equips engineering leaders to unlock their team's innovation potential.

STRATEGIES FOR CULTIVATING INNOVATIVE THINKING

Fostering an innovative culture is essential for high-performance in engineering, yet doing so dynamically brings both opportunities and challenges. This section provides strategies to cultivate the creative thinking that drives innovation, while navigating difficulties that may arise.

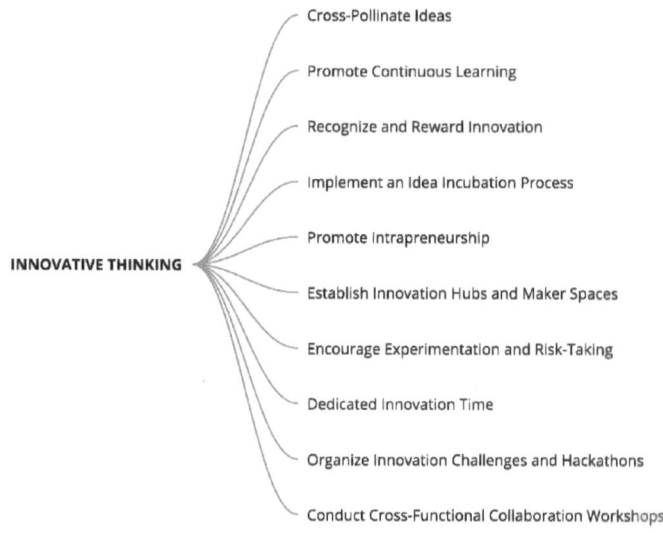

(1) *Dedicated Innovation Time*: Set aside regular work hours for unstructured creative exploration and experimentation.
   - Block off Fridays from 1-3pm for "Innovation Lab" - time to experiment with no set expectations.
   - Encourage hackathons during the Innovation Lab where people self-organize around new ideas.
   - Maintain an online "Innovation Wall" for team members to post and discuss creative ideas.
(2) *Conduct Cross-Functional Collaboration Workshops*: Foster innovation through interactive sessions for teams to solve problems together.
   - Host quarterly 2-day offsite workshops for cross-team problem solving.
   - Structure sessions with design thinking exercises and rapid prototyping.
   - Assign interdisciplinary teams to tackle real company challenges.

(3) *Organize Innovation Challenges and Hackathons*: Drive rapid ideation and unconventional solutions through constrained competitions.

- Hold a virtual 24-hour hackathon focused on green initiatives. Offer prizes for top ideas.
- Pose an innovation challenge around improving customer retention. Give teams a month to develop solutions.

(4) *Promote Intrapreneurship*: Support internal entrepreneurial initiatives aligned to company goals.

- Allocate seed funding for team members to self-organize and launch validated idea pilots.
- Assign innovation mentors to help teams develop concepts, business cases, and MVPs.

(5) *Encourage Experimentation and Risk-Taking*: Cultivate a culture that embraces bold experimentation and learns from failures.

- Encourage rapid prototyping of new ideas using low-fidelity mocks rather than polished specs.
- Celebrate brave but failed experiments during retros as valuable learning opportunities.

(6) *Establish Innovation Hubs and Maker Spaces*: Provide collaborative environments with tools to prototype and test ideas.

- Create a physical Innovation Lab equipped with whiteboards, post-its, arts supplies, and tech tools.
- Stock virtual collaboration spaces with design thinking templates, ideation guides, and prototyping software.

(7) *Cross-Pollinate Ideas*: Facilitate knowledge sharing across teams to blend diverse perspectives.

- Organize rotating lunch-and-learn sessions for different teams to share challenges and ideas.
- Maintain cross-functional Slack channels as ongoing forums to exchange insights.

(8) *Promote Continuous Learning*: Foster constant growth mindset through exposure to emerging trends.

- Sponsor conferences and workshops related to emerging technologies.

- Implement perpetual beta philosophy of always improving.

(9) *Implement an Idea Incubation Process*: Provide structured support to develop top concepts from ideation to execution.

- Host quarterly innovation pitch events for teams to get feedback on developing concepts.
- Provide dedicated resources like time, budget, and mentors to incubate top ideas.

(10) *Recognize and Reward Innovation*: Spotlight and incentivize impactful innovations through formal programs.

- Feature successful innovations in company newsletters and events.
- Incorporate innovation impact into performance reviews and advancement criteria.

While the strategies for building a high-performance engineering team often emphasize skill development and project execution, strategies for cultivating an innovative culture focus on creating an environment that nurtures creativity, idea generation, and a continuous pursuit of groundbreaking solutions.

OVERCOMING CHALLENGES TO FOSTERING INNOVATIVE THINKING

Cultivating an innovative culture within high-performance engineering teams is a transformative journey that brings immense value, but it's not without its challenges. Effectively addressing these challenges is crucial to ensure that the team can navigate obstacles and sustain an environment conducive to continuous innovation. In this section, we explore strategies to overcome common challenges associated with fostering an innovative culture, providing insights to guide teams toward sustained creativity and high performance.

THE TEN TRAITS OF HIGH PERFORMING ENGINEERING TEAMS

(1) *Resistance to Change*: Team members may resist adopting new innovative practices or changes to existing workflows.

- *Strategy*: Communicate the benefits of an innovative culture clearly, emphasizing personal and collective growth. Involve the team in decision-making processes to increase buy-in and facilitate a smoother transition. Showcase success stories where innovative thinking led to positive outcomes.

(2) *Fear of Failure*: A fear of failure can hinder the willingness to take risks and experiment with new ideas.

- *Strategy*: Foster a culture that views failures as opportunities for learning and improvement. Celebrate lessons learned from unsuccessful attempts and emphasize that failure is a natural part of the innovation process.

(3) *Resource Constraints*: Limited resources, including time and budget, may pose challenges to implementing comprehensive innovation programs.

- *Strategy*: Advocate for additional resources by showcasing the long-term benefits of innovation. Prioritize innovation initiatives based on their impact and relevance to current and future projects. Explore creative solutions that require minimal resources but yield significant innovation.

(4) *Lack of Structured Innovation Processes*: The absence of structured processes for nurturing and implementing innovative ideas can lead to ad-hoc approaches.

- *Strategy*: Establish a structured innovation framework that includes ideation, evaluation, prototyping, and implementation stages. Provide training on the innovation process to ensure that all team members understand and can contribute effectively.

(5) *Siloed Work Environments*: Silos within the team can hinder cross-functional collaboration, limiting the exchange of innovative ideas.

- *Strategy*: Implement cross-functional collaboration initiatives, encourage interdisciplinary interactions, and utilize project management tools that facilitate transparent communication across all team members. Foster a culture that values and promotes collaboration across different functional areas.

(6) *Inadequate Recognition for Innovation*: The lack of recognition for innovative contributions may demotivate team members.

- *Strategy*: Implement a robust recognition system that acknowledges and celebrates innovative achievements. Showcase success stories and highlight the positive impact of innovative thinking on project outcomes and overall team success.

(7) *Leadership Alignment*: Lack of alignment from leadership on the importance of innovation can impact the team's commitment to creative endeavors.

- *Strategy*: Actively involve leadership in innovation initiatives, emphasizing the strategic value of innovation in achieving organizational goals. Encourage leaders to communicate the importance of innovation and model innovative behaviors.

(8) *Balancing Short-Term Goals with Long-Term Innovation*: Pressure for immediate results may overshadow the long-term benefits of continuous innovation.

- *Strategy*: Communicate the long-term value of innovation initiatives. Showcase examples where innovative thinking has led to groundbreaking solutions and improved project outcomes. Balance short-term goals with strategic, long-term innovation planning.

(9) *Lack of Diverse Perspectives*: Homogeneous teams may struggle to generate a wide range of innovative ideas.

- *Strategy*: Actively promote diversity within the team and create an inclusive environment where all perspectives are valued. Encourage diverse teams to collaborate on innovation projects to leverage a variety of insights.

(10) *Technological Barriers*: Inadequate or unfamiliar technology can hinder the implementation of innovative solutions.

- *Strategy*: Invest in user-friendly collaborative technologies, provide comprehensive training on their usage, and encourage ongoing exploration of new tools that enhance innovation and collaboration.

By proactively addressing these challenges and implementing tailored strategies, high-performance engineering teams can create an innovative culture that not only overcomes obstacles but also thrives in the face of complex engineering projects. It's a continuous process of adaptation and improvement, ensuring that the innovative culture remains a driving force behind the team's success.

7

AGILE AND ADAPTABLE

In today's fast-changing technology landscape, adaptability is critical to engineering success. But how can teams stay nimble and responsive? This chapter shows leaders how to build agile cultures ready to flex and adjust to dynamic business conditions.

Readers will learn frameworks like Scrum and Lean that empower teams to iterate quickly based on user feedback. The chapter explores strategies for decentralizing authority, allowing autonomy, and spurring creativity so engineers can rapidly prototype and test solutions.

Engineers will gain insight into leading indicators that signal when processes or structures need to evolve to meet emerging challenges. By mastering tactics to instill agility and continuously adapt, engineering teams can accelerate innovation, reduce wasted effort, and deliver more value, more often.

STRATEGIES FOR CULTIVATING AGILITY AND ADAPTABILITY

Cultivating agility and adaptability is essential to navigate the ever-changing landscape of challenges and opportunities. The following strategies provide a roadmap for engineering teams to foster agility and adaptability, ensuring they not only respond effectively to change but also proactively shape their environment for continued success:

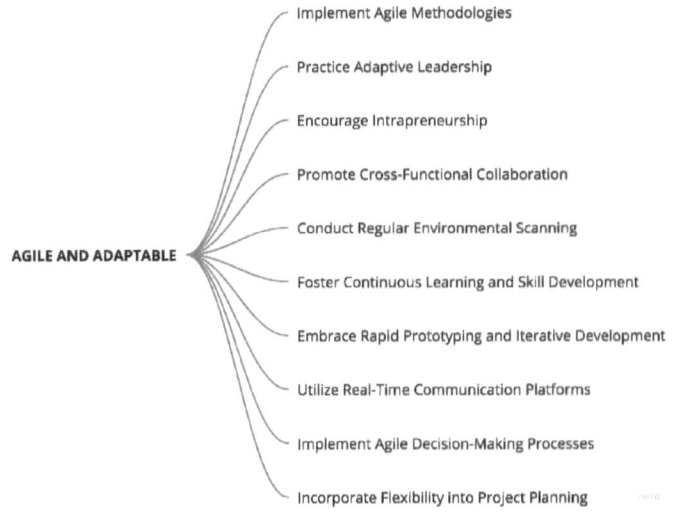

AGILE AND ADAPTABLE
- Implement Agile Methodologies
- Practice Adaptive Leadership
- Encourage Intrapreneurship
- Promote Cross-Functional Collaboration
- Conduct Regular Environmental Scanning
- Foster Continuous Learning and Skill Development
- Embrace Rapid Prototyping and Iterative Development
- Utilize Real-Time Communication Platforms
- Implement Agile Decision-Making Processes
- Incorporate Flexibility into Project Planning

(1) *Implement Agile Methodologies*: Adopt iterative approaches for faster delivery and responsiveness to change.
- Conduct daily 15 minute standup meetings for project status updates and blocker identification.
- Organize retrospectives after each biweekly sprint to discuss what worked well and areas for improvement.
- Use story pointing techniques like planning poker to collectively estimate work effort.

(2) *Promote Cross-Functional Collaboration*: Integrate diverse expertise across disciplines to enable adaptability.
- Structure regular "lunch and learn" sessions for engineers across disciplines to share knowledge.
- Assign cross-functional pairs to collaborate on key project features.
- Organize hackathons periodically for creative cross-pollination.

(3) *Embrace Rapid Prototyping and Iterative Development*: Accelerate innovation through fast testing and refinement cycles.

- Structure design sprints focused on rapid ideation and user testing.
- Prioritize minimum viable product (MVP) development over polished products.
- Gather user feedback frequently and refine prototypes in short iterations.

(4) *Foster Continuous Learning and Skill Development*: Keep teams relevant through constant exposure to new skills and ideas.

- Sponsor relevant conferences, workshops, and courses aligned to project needs.
- Set time aside weekly for self-directed learning and skill sharpening.
- Develop personalized annual training plans during performance reviews.

(5) *Practice Adaptive Leadership*: Equip leaders to guide teams through uncertainty and change.

- Train managers in change management models like ADKAR.
- Conduct regular anonymous surveys to gather team feedback.
- Empower managers to adapt goals and timelines based on evolving needs.

(6) *Conduct Regular Environmental Scanning*: Monitor external trends and events impacting projects.

- Designate a team to monitor emerging technologies and trends full-time.
- Subscribe to industry reports and publications for ongoing updates.
- Share key findings and impacts during monthly all-hands meetings.

(7) *Encourage Intrapreneurship*: Support internal innovation aligned to company needs.

- Allocate working hours each week for employees to experiment with new ideas or tools.
- Organize quarterly hackathons to showcase innovative personal projects.
- Provide seed funding for high-potential ventures aligned to company goals.

(8) *Utilize Real-Time Communication Platforms*: Enable instant coordination through digital channels.

- Require all team members to install and routinely use Slack and Teams apps.
- Document and share conventions for using channels effectively.
- Train employees on providing quick responses during work hours.

(9) *Implement Agile Decision-Making Processes*: Decide fast, implement, gather feedback, and adjust.

- Default to verbal discussion over drawn-out documentation wherever possible.
- Empower project leads to make on-the-spot decisions independently.
- Implement voting techniques to resolve disputes efficiently.

(10) *Incorporate Flexibility into Project Planning*: Build in buffers to accommodate changing timelines and priorities.

- Build in buffer time for unexpected tasks.
- Define priorities to allow for de-scoping if needed.
- Review and revise plans at least monthly with core project team.

By weaving these strategies into the fabric of high-performance engineering teams, organizations can cultivate a culture where agility and adaptability are not just reactive measures but ingrained qualities that propel the team forward amidst uncertainty and change.

OVERCOMING CHALLENGES TO AGILITY AND ADAPTABILITY

Realizing the benefits of agile and adaptable engineering cultures brings leadership challenges that must be addressed. This section provides techniques to anticipate and mitigate these challenges while still empowering autonomous teams to pivot quickly. By highlighting potential pitfalls, leaders can proactively cultivate adaptive cultures that balance agility with order and discipline.

(1) *Resistance to Change*: Some team members may resist adopting new agile methodologies or adapting to changes in workflows.
- *Strategy*: Clearly communicate the benefits of agility, emphasizing personal and collective growth. Involve the team in decision-making processes to increase buy-in, and showcase success stories where adaptability led to positive outcomes.

(2) *Silos and Departmental Barriers*: Silos within the team or across departments can hinder seamless collaboration and adaptive responses to change.
- *Strategy*: Implement cross-functional collaboration initiatives, encourage knowledge sharing, and establish interdisciplinary teams. Foster a culture that values and promotes collaboration across different functional areas.

(3) *Ineffective Communication Channels*: Ineffective communication channels can result in misunderstandings and hinder the free flow of information.
- *Strategy*: Establish clear communication channels, utilize collaborative tools for real-time updates, and conduct regular training on effective communication. Implement guidelines for communication etiquette to streamline information exchange.

(4) *Lack of Leadership Support*: Lack of support or modeling of agile and adaptive behaviors by leadership can impact team culture.

- *Strategy*: Actively involve leadership in agile initiatives, emphasize the importance of agility in achieving organizational goals, and provide training for leadership on fostering an adaptive culture.

(5) *Balancing Stability and Adaptability*: Striking the right balance between maintaining stability and embracing adaptability can be challenging.

- *Strategy*: Communicate the importance of adaptability in responding to changing project needs. Implement flexible project planning methodologies that allow adjustments without compromising overall stability.

(6) *Team Dynamics and Trust Issues*: Building trust among team members, especially in virtual or distributed team setups, can be challenging.

- *Strategy*: Organize team-building activities, encourage open feedback sessions, and establish a culture of accountability. Foster an environment where team members feel comfortable sharing ideas and collaborating without fear of judgment.

(7) *Overcoming Technological Barriers*: Inadequate or unfamiliar collaborative tools can hinder effective virtual teamwork.

- *Strategy*: Invest in user-friendly collaborative technologies, provide comprehensive training on their usage, and encourage ongoing exploration of new tools that enhance virtual collaboration.

(8) *Measuring and Recognizing Agility*: It may be challenging to measure and recognize the agile efforts of team members.

- *Strategy*: Implement performance metrics that reflect agile contributions, recognize and celebrate adaptive achievements, and tie agility to performance evaluations. Showcase examples where agility led to project success.

(9) *Evolving Skill Set*: Team members may need to acquire new skills for embracing agile methodologies.

- *Strategy*: Provide targeted training programs and resources to enhance the team's skill set. Encourage a culture of continuous learning, where team members actively seek opportunities to acquire and apply new skills.

(10) *Adapting to Remote Work Challenges*: Remote or distributed teams may face additional challenges in coordinating real-time collaboration.

- *Strategy*: Establish clear guidelines for remote collaboration, utilize asynchronous communication tools, and provide support for overcoming time zone differences. Implement flexible scheduling options to accommodate the unique dynamics of remote teams.

By addressing these challenges proactively and implementing tailored strategies, high-performance engineering teams can navigate the complexities of cultivating agility and adaptability. It's an ongoing process of learning and adaptation, ensuring that the team remains resilient and responsive to the ever-evolving landscape of engineering projects.

8

RESULT-DRIVEN FOCUS

The intricate nature of modern engineering projects demands more than technical prowess; it necessitates a laser-sharp focus on results that goes beyond individual brilliance. This chapter unravels the key strategies and principles that underpin a results-driven culture, emphasizing the critical role it plays in steering teams toward unparalleled success.

From setting clear and measurable goals to implementing agile methodologies, from data-driven decision-making to fostering a results-driven mindset, each strategy outlined in this chapter serves as a compass guiding engineering teams toward the pinnacle of performance. The focus on achieving tangible outcomes aligns individual efforts with overarching project goals, creating a culture where success is not just an aspiration but a measurable reality.

As we delve into the strategies that define a results-driven culture, it becomes evident that this focus is more than a methodology – it's a commitment to excellence that permeates every facet of the team's endeavors. Join us in exploring how engineering teams can harness the power of a results-driven mindset to navigate the complexities of modern projects, ensuring that each effort contributes meaningfully to the overarching success of the team.

STRATEGIES FOR CULTIVATING A RESULT DRIVEN CULTURE

Cultivating a results-driven culture within a high-performance engineering team involves intentional strategies that focus on achieving measurable outcomes and continuous improvement. Here are key strategies for fostering a results-driven culture:

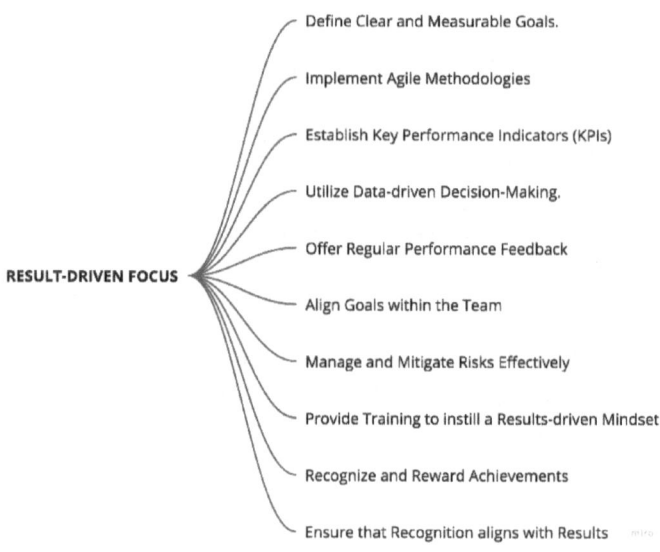

RESULT-DRIVEN FOCUS
- Define Clear and Measurable Goals.
- Implement Agile Methodologies
- Establish Key Performance Indicators (KPIs)
- Utilize Data-driven Decision-Making.
- Offer Regular Performance Feedback
- Align Goals within the Team
- Manage and Mitigate Risks Effectively
- Provide Training to instill a Results-driven Mindset
- Recognize and Reward Achievements
- Ensure that Recognition aligns with Results

(1) *Define Clear and Measurable Goals*: Define specific, quantified, time-bound goals collaboratively.
- Set quantified goals for key metrics like uptime, defects, velocity, and net promoter score.
- Make goals time-bound and assign owners accountable for each goal.
- Ensure goals are realistic yet ambitious enough to drive results.

(2) *Establish Key Performance Indicators (KPIs)*: Identify quantifiable metrics to objectively track progress on goals.

- Identify 3-5 KPIs directly tied to critical goals, like lead generation and customer retention rates.
- Display KPI dashboards at standups and monitor trends over time.
- Establish targets for each KPI to objectively track progress.

(3) *Implement Agile Methodologies*: Adopt agile practices like Scrum to deliver results iteratively.

- Adopt agile practices like Scrum to deliver results iteratively at a sustainable pace.
- Utilize daily standups, retrospectives, and sprint reviews to frequently inspect and adapt.
- Ensure backlogs are prioritized by value to align with goals.

(4) *Utilize Data-driven Decision-making*: Leverage data and metrics to guide priorities and roadmaps.

- Leverage data from KPIs, A/B tests, and customer analytics to guide roadmaps.
- Require data analysis when proposing new features or strategic objectives.
- Train teams on extracting insights from data.

(5) *Offer Regular Performance Feedback*: Conduct consistent reviews tied to results and development areas.

- Conduct quarterly reviews 1-on-1s tied to progress on goals and development areas.
- Seek informal peer feedback on contributions to team results.
- Incorporate goal progress into performance management.

(6) *Align Goals within the Team*: Ensure individual goals trace back to core organizational objectives.

- Cascade top-level company goals into team and individual goals to connect to broader objectives.

- Ensure all projects and initiatives can be tied directly to critical goals. Decline or deprioritize other efforts.
- Provide visibility into how each person's work impacts overarching goals.

(7) *Provide Training to instill a Results-driven Mindset*: Train teams on techniques for focus, prioritization, and goal achievement.

- Conduct workshops on techniques for focusing efforts, prioritizing effectively, and goal achievement.
- Share case studies and examples highlighting impact of results focus.
- Offer online courses and resources on goal setting, productivity, and time management.

(8) *Manage and Mitigate Risks Effectively*: Proactively identify and plan for risks that could impede results.

- Maintain a risk register updated with probability, impact, status, and mitigation actions.
- Identify risks proactively through regular analysis of upcoming initiatives.
- Conduct contingency planning exercises for high priority risks.

(9) *Recognize and Reward Achievements*: Celebrate teams and individuals who successfully complete milestones.

- Call out wins and milestones in team meetings and company newsletters.
- Develop Wall of Success showcasing major goal achievement.
- Structure bonus programs and advancement criteria tied to results.

(10) *Ensure that Recognition aligns with Results*: Reinforce behaviors that contribute to measurable outcomes.

- Praise specific behaviors that contribute to goal progress like collaboration and creativity.
- Avoid recognition lacking ties to outcomes.
- Spotlight impact of top contributors on wins through storytelling.

By implementing these strategies, engineering teams can create a results-driven culture that not only emphasizes achieving outcomes but also encourages continuous learning, innovation, and adaptability. This culture becomes a driving force behind the team's high performance and sustained success in meeting organizational objectives.

OVERCOMING CHALLENGES TO ACHIEVING RESULTS-DRIVEN OUTCOMES

Overcoming challenges in cultivating a results-driven culture for a high-performance engineering team requires addressing potential obstacles that may impede progress toward goals. Here are strategies to navigate and overcome common challenges associated with fostering a results-driven culture:

(1) *Unclear or Ambiguous Goals*: Unclear or ambiguous project objectives can hinder the team's ability to set and achieve measurable goals.
   - *Strategy*: Invest time in collaborative goal-setting sessions, ensuring that objectives are specific, measurable, achievable, relevant, and time-bound (SMART). Regularly revisit and clarify goals as needed, keeping the entire team aligned with project expectations.
(2) *Inadequate Performance Measurement*: Defining KPIs that do not accurately reflect project success can lead to misinterpretation of performance.
   - *Strategy*: Engage the team in the selection of relevant KPIs that directly contribute to project outcomes. Regularly assess and refine KPIs based on the evolving nature of the project and its objectives.
(3) *Resistance to Change*: Introducing a results-driven culture may face resistance from team members accustomed to traditional approaches.
   - *Strategy*: Communicate the benefits of a results-driven mindset clearly, emphasizing personal and team

growth. Involve team members in the decision-making process and showcase success stories where a results-driven approach led to positive outcomes.

(4) *Client and Stakeholder Misalignment*: Misalignment with client expectations or stakeholder priorities can result in a disconnect between perceived and actual project success.

- *Strategy*: Schedule regular check-ins with clients to discuss expectations and obtain feedback. Establish a collaborative platform for stakeholders to share their perspectives, ensuring that project goals align with broader organizational objectives.

(5) *Lack of Individual Ownership*: A lack of individual ownership can impede progress as team members may not feel personally responsible for project outcomes.

- *Strategy*: Implement regular one-on-one sessions between team members and project leaders to discuss individual roles and contributions. Establish a system where each team member sets personal goals aligned with project objectives. Recognize and celebrate instances where individual ownership has directly impacted project success.

(6) *Insufficient Recognition and Rewards*: Inadequate recognition and rewards may lead to demotivation and a lack of enthusiasm among team members.

- Strategy: Develop a tiered recognition system where achievements are acknowledged through a combination of public praise, tangible rewards, and career development opportunities. Create a structured feedback loop to gather input on the effectiveness of the recognition system, and make adjustments accordingly.

(7) *Communication Barriers*: Communication barriers can hinder the exchange of critical information and impede collaborative efforts.

- *Strategy*: Implement a standardized communication protocol specifying channels for different types of information. Provide communication training sessions focused on active listening and clear expression. Foster a culture of open communication where team members feel comfortable raising concerns and providing feedback.

(8) *Inconsistent Feedback*: Inconsistent feedback may lead to a lack of clarity regarding individual and team performance.

- *Strategy*: Establish a bi-monthly feedback schedule, ensuring that every team member receives constructive input on their performance. Provide training on delivering specific and actionable feedback. Integrate feedback discussions into regular project review meetings to align feedback with project outcomes.

(9) *Lack of Alignment with Organizational Values*: A lack of alignment with organizational values may result in a disconnect between team objectives and broader organizational goals.

- *Strategy*: Develop an organizational values handbook outlining how each value translates into specific behaviors within the engineering team. Integrate discussions about organizational values into regular team meetings. Recognize and reward instances where team members embody these values in their project contributions.

(10) *Overemphasis on Short-Term Results*: Overemphasis on short-term results may neglect long-term objectives and sustainability.

- *Strategy*: Implement a quarterly strategic planning session where the team collectively discusses both short-term goals and long-term objectives. Develop key milestones for the next quarter while keeping an eye on the broader project vision. Integrate long-term success metrics into performance evaluations.

By proactively addressing these challenges, high-performance engineering teams can pave the way for a results-driven culture that not only overcomes obstacles but thrives in the pursuit of ambitious goals. Continuous adaptation, learning, and a commitment to improvement form the bedrock of a culture that consistently delivers exceptional results.

9

Resilience in the Face of Challenges

Setbacks and failures are inevitable in complex technology projects. But how can leaders foster cultures ready to persist in the face of challenges? This chapter reveals techniques to strengthen engineering teams with the resilience to recover and press forward when plans go awry.

Readers will explore strategies for normalizing failure as a learning opportunity, leveraging lessons from past stumbles, and acknowledging uncertainties from the start. The chapter provides frameworks for emotionally intelligent leadership and open communication that equips teams to constructively problem-solve when projects hit roadblocks.

Engineers will learn the art of bouncing back through concrete practices like conducting proactive post-mortems, running failure drills, and emphasizing process over outcomes. By mastering tools to build resilience, leaders can empower teams to view obstacles as chances to iterate and improve.

With the mindsets and methods this chapter provides, engineering organizations can develop the systemic resilience to absorb setbacks, adapt, and continue driving toward success in the turbulence of complex technical environments. Readers will walk away better able to lead teams that learn from failures, pivot after missteps, and persist through crises.

STRATEGIES FOR CULTIVATING RESILIENCE

Cultivating resilience is imperative for high-performance engineering teams facing the complexities and uncertainties of modern projects. Resilience enables teams to navigate challenges effectively, learn from setbacks, and continuously improve. Here are strategic approaches to foster resilience within your engineering team:

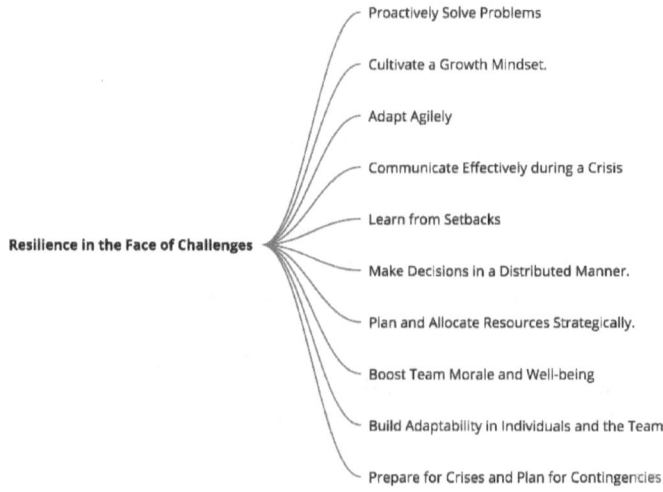

Resilience in the Face of Challenges
- Proactively Solve Problems
- Cultivate a Growth Mindset.
- Adapt Agilely
- Communicate Effectively during a Crisis
- Learn from Setbacks
- Make Decisions in a Distributed Manner.
- Plan and Allocate Resources Strategically.
- Boost Team Morale and Well-being
- Build Adaptability in Individuals and the Team
- Prepare for Crises and Plan for Contingencies

(1) *Proactively Solve Problems*: Anticipate and prevent problems before they occur.
   - Conduct regular risk assessments to identify vulnerabilities.
   - Put monitoring systems in place to detect issues early.
   - Define escalation protocols for emerging problems.
(2) *Cultivate a Growth Mindset*: Foster a culture of learning from failures and challenges.
   - Train managers on giving effective feedback that focuses on effort and improvement.

- Reward attempts and celebrate progress even if goals weren't fully met.
- Encourage sharing lessons learned from failures.

(3) *Communicate Effectively during a Crisis:* Clear, timely, and transparent communication is key during crises.

- Create pre-defined crisis response plan with stakeholders and channels.
- Designate spokespeople and equip with talking points.
- Overcommunicate during turbulent times

(4) *Adapt Agilely:* Build in flexibility to pivot plans when needed.

- Build slack into schedules to allow for uncertainty.
- Modularize workstreams for adjustable scope.
- Empower teams to rapidly respond to changing conditions.

(5) *Learn from Setbacks:* Analyze major setbacks to identify improvements.

- Conduct blameless postmortems after major incidents.
- Feed findings into preventative measures and training
- Publicize key learnings across organization.

(6) *Make Decisions in a Distributed Manner:* Empower teams to make contextual real-time decisions.

- Define escalation paths and thresholds for decisions.
- Provide visibility into real-time data and context.
- Solicit input from different levels during crisis.

(7) *Plan and Allocate Resources strategically:* Proactively manage resources and have contingency plans.

- Maintain capacity buffers and contingency plans.
- Cross-train team members to enable flexible resource allocation.
- Keep tab on emerging resource needs and gaps.

(8) *Boost Team Morale and Well-being:* Prioritize psychological safety and prevent burnout.

- Check in frequently and address mental health concerns.
- Allow time for people to recharge and recover.

- Celebrate examples of resilience post-crisis
(9) *Build Adaptability in Individuals and the Team*: Prioritize
psychological safety and prevent burnout.
  - Vary exposure to challenges and projects.
  - Foster learning agility through mentorship and training
  - Reward those who adapt best to uncertain conditions.
(10) *Prepare for Crises and Plan for Contingencies*: Prepare for
crises through training and redundancies.
  - War game various crisis scenarios
  - Solidify crisis response protocols and systems.
  - Maintain redundant systems and backups of critical
    resources.

The ability to anticipate challenges, learn from failures,
adapt swiftly, communicate effectively, and boost morale in
times of crisis allows organizations to minimize disruptions
and continuously improve. While cultivating resilience
requires investment, it pays long-term dividends through
enhanced performance.

OVERCOMING CHALLENGES TO BUILDING A RESILIENT-DRIVEN CULTURE

Maintaining resilience is a crucial aspect of high-performance
engineering teams, especially when facing unforeseen
challenges. Here are key strategies to cultivate resilience and
ensure teams can bounce back effectively:

(1) *Proactive Crisis Preparedness*: Unexpected crises can disrupt
workflow and impact team morale.
  - *Strategy*: Develop crisis response plans that outline
    roles and responsibilities. Conduct regular drills to
    ensure the team is well-prepared for various scenarios.
    Establish clear communication channels during crises
    to disseminate information efficiently.
(2) *Adaptability to Change*: Rapid changes in project
requirements or external factors can be stressful.

- *Strategy*: Foster an adaptable mindset within the team. Encourage openness to change and provide training on agile methodologies. Establish a feedback loop for continuous improvement based on lessons learned from adapting to previous challenges.

(3) *Team Cohesion During Turbulence*: Turbulent periods may strain team dynamics and collaboration.

- *Strategy*: Strengthen team bonds through team-building activities and regular check-ins. Foster a culture of support and open communication. Emphasize the shared goal of overcoming challenges together to instill a sense of unity.

(4) *Individual and Collective Stress Management*: High-pressure situations can lead to stress and burnout.

- *Strategy*: Provide resources for stress management, such as workshops or counseling services. Encourage team members to take breaks and prioritize self-care. Promote a healthy work-life balance to prevent prolonged stress.

(5) *Learning from Setbacks*: Failures or setbacks can be demoralizing without a constructive approach.

- *Strategy*: Cultivate a culture that views setbacks as opportunities for learning and improvement. Conduct post-mortem analyses after challenging projects to identify lessons learned and implement changes for future resilience.

(6) *Transparent Leadership Communication*: Lack of transparent communication from leadership can create uncertainty.

- Strategy: Maintain open and honest communication channels. Keep the team informed about challenges and progress. Provide a clear vision for navigating through adversity and emphasize the collective strength of the team.

(7) *Flexibility Arrangements in Work*: External factors, such as a global crisis, may require changes in work arrangements.

- *Strategy*: Establish flexible work policies to accommodate unforeseen circumstances. Provide remote work options and technological support for seamless collaboration. Communicate expectations clearly to maintain productivity.

(8) *Continuous Skill Development*: Rapid technological advancements may require new skills.

- *Strategy*: Encourage continuous learning and upskilling. Provide resources for online courses and certifications. Foster a culture that values adaptability and the acquisition of new skills to enhance the team's overall resilience.

(9) *Celebrating Resilience and Milestones*: The resilience of the team might go unnoticed during challenging times.

- *Strategy*: Acknowledge and celebrate the team's resilience during and after challenging periods. Recognize individual and collective efforts. This positive reinforcement reinforces the importance of resilience.

(10) *Building a Support Network*: Team members may feel isolated during difficult times.

- *Strategy*: Establish support networks within the team. Encourage mentorship and peer support. Provide resources for mental health and create a safe space for open discussions about challenges and coping strategies.

By implementing these strategies, high-performance engineering teams can cultivate resilience, enabling them to navigate challenges with strength and adaptability. This focus on resilience contributes to the overall sustainability and success of the team in the face of adversity.

10

Passionate Engagement

Inspiring passionate commitment from teams separates good engineering leaders from great ones. But how can managers spark such fervor? This chapter reveals techniques to foster engaged, motivated cultures ready to pour their hearts into their work.

Readers will explore strategies for connecting engineering efforts to compelling missions that provide meaning and purpose. The chapter provides frameworks for empowering teams with autonomy, mastery, and progress to drive passionate participation.

With the methods this chapter details, engineering organizations can develop self-organizing teams intrinsically motivated to drive innovations. Leaders will walk away better equipped to lead engaged teams that bring energy, initiative, and passion to their technology work.

STRATEGIES FOR CULTIVATING PASSIONATE ENGAGEMENT

Passionate engagement is a driving force behind the success of high-performance engineering teams. When team members are deeply connected to their work, they not only meet expectations but exceed them, contributing to a culture of innovation and excellence. Cultivating this level of passion requires intentional strategies that go beyond task completion. Here are key approaches to foster passionate engagement within your engineering team:

(1) *Align Purposes Purposefully*: Connect work to a meaningful mission.
  - Connect projects to company mission and values.
  - Highlight positive impact on customers and society.
  - Share customer feedback and testimonials.
(2) *Grant Autonomy and Ownership*: Empower teams with responsibility and authority.
  - Allow teams to drive solutions and set timelines.
  - Provide decision-making authority and trust their expertise.
  - Solicit input on processes and policies.
(3) *Pose Meaningful Challenges*: Match projects to team capabilities and interests.
  - Ensure technical scope fully leverages team capabilities.
  - Provide opportunities to learn new skills and tools.

- Vary complexity across projects.

(4) *Recognize and Appreciate*: Celebrate both big and small accomplishments.

- Celebrate project milestones and wins.
- Recognize efforts both big and small.
- Customize rewards based on team motivations.

(5) *Offer Professional Growth Opportunities*: Provide advancement, training, and development.

- Offer tuition reimbursement and learning stipends.
- Develop clear promotion tracks.
- Support conferences, training, mentors

(6) *Cultivate a Collaborative Environment*: Promote teamwork, idea sharing, and social connections.

- Encourage idea sharing and brainstorming.
- Provide spaces for informal collaboration.
- Organize networking events and socials.

(7) *Establish Innovation Platforms*: Offer ways to experiment and pursue original ideas.

- Establish hackathons, 20% time, labs.
- Reward successful experiments
- Crowdsource ideas from the team.

(8) *Set Goals Clearly*: Define shared objectives and success metrics.

- Co-define success metrics and project scope.
- Establish milestones and celebrate progress.
- Revisit goals frequently

(9) *Provide Regular Feedback and Development Plans*: Give coaching and create growth plans.

- Set up recurring 1:1s and check-ins.
- Create personalized development plans.
- Coach managers to have growth-focused conversations.

(10) *Support Flexibility and Work-life Balance*: Allow flexible scheduling and respect personal time.

- Offer flexible schedules and remote work options.
- Discourage after-hours work patterns.

- Respect and protect personal time.

Cultivating passionate engagement is an ongoing process that involves understanding individual motivations, fostering a supportive culture, and providing opportunities for growth and impact. By implementing these strategies, high-performance engineering teams can create an environment where passion thrives, leading to exceptional outcomes and sustained success.

OVERCOMING CHALLENGES TO FOSTERING PASSIONATE ENGAGEMENT

While cultivating passionate engagement is a powerful catalyst for high-performance engineering teams, challenges may arise that require thoughtful solutions. Addressing these challenges proactively ensures that the flame of passion continues to burn brightly within the team. Here are strategies to overcome common challenges associated with fostering passionate engagement:

1. *Mismatched Job Roles and Interests*: Team members may feel disengaged if their job roles do not align with their interests.
    1. *Strategy*: Conduct regular discussions to understand individual interests and aspirations. Adjust job roles or allocate tasks that align with the passions of team members, ensuring a more fulfilling work experience.
2. *Limited Resources for Passion Projects*: Constraints on time, budget, or resources may hinder the pursuit of passion-driven projects.
    1. *Strategy*: Advocate for dedicated resources for passion projects. Prioritize initiatives that align with individual and team interests,

and emphasize the long-term benefits of fostering passion within the team.

3. *Communication Barriers*: Ineffective communication can lead to misunderstandings, hindering the conveyance of passion and enthusiasm.

   1. *Strategy*: Implement clear communication channels and practices. Encourage team members to express their passions openly, and ensure that leadership actively listens and responds to their ideas and concerns.

4. *Burnout and Overwhelm*: Excessive workloads or unrealistic expectations can lead to burnout, diminishing passion.

   1. *Strategy*: Monitor workloads and promote a healthy work-life balance. Provide support, delegate tasks when necessary, and create an environment where team members feel comfortable expressing concerns about workload.

5. *Lack of Recognition*: Insufficient recognition may demotivate team members, leading to reduced passion.

   1. *Strategy*: Enhance the recognition system to ensure that individual and team achievements are acknowledged consistently. Recognize efforts in a personalized manner, considering the preferences of each team member.

6. *Resistance to Change*: Team members may resist changes that impact their routines, affecting their engagement levels.

   1. *Strategy*: Communicate the benefits of change clearly and involve the team in decision-making processes. Emphasize how changes contribute to a more passionate and innovative work environment.

7. *Limited Growth Opportunities*: Perceived stagnation in career growth may lead to disengagement.

1. *Strategy*: Provide opportunities for skill development, career advancement, and new challenges. Create individualized growth plans aligned with the aspirations of team members, fostering a sense of continuous development.

8. *Unclear Path for Passion Pursuit*: Team members may struggle to see a clear path for integrating their passions into their work.

   1. *Strategy*: Facilitate discussions to explore how individual passions can be incorporated into projects. Establish mentorship programs or interest-based teams to provide guidance and support for pursuing passions.

9. *Leadership Misalignment*: Misalignment between leadership and team values can impact the overall passion culture.

   1. *Strategy*: Ensure that leadership actively supports and participates in initiatives to foster passion. Align leadership actions and communication with the values and goals that promote passionate engagement.

10. *Inadequate Training and Skill Development*: Lack of opportunities for skill enhancement may hinder the pursuit of passions that require specific expertise.

1. *Strategy*: Invest in training programs that align with the skills needed for passion-driven projects. Provide resources and support for acquiring new skills, enabling team members to pursue their passions effectively.

By actively addressing these challenges, high-performance engineering teams can create a resilient foundation for passionate engagement. The strategies outlined above not only mitigate potential obstacles but also contribute to the sustained cultivation of a passionate culture that fuels innovation, creativity, and collective success.

Conclusion

The landscape of engineering leadership is dynamic and complex. Through the journey of this guide, we have charted a path through ten pivotal principles to steer teams toward high performance. As we conclude, let's reflect on the key lessons to lead engineering teams that innovate boldly, adapt resiliently, achieve results, and engage with passion.

HOLISTIC LEADERSHIP

Success requires technical expertise complemented by strategic thinking, emotional intelligence, and an ability to motivate. By embracing a multifaceted approach, leaders empower teams to navigate challenges and rapidly adapt.

DRIVING INNOVATION

Cultivating creative cultures is vital to progress. Leaders must foster environments where imagination thrives, failure leads to learning, and teams feel inspired to push boundaries.

RESULTS-FOCUSED EXECUTION

Progress demands aligning efforts to outcomes. Leaders must implement clear goals, data-driven decisions, and proactive risk management to achieve consistent results.

RESILIENCE THROUGH CHALLENGES

Setbacks are inevitable. By promoting failure as growth, transparent communication, and adaptive resource planning, leaders build resilience to rebound from crises.

PASSIONATE ENGAGEMENT

Passion separates good teams from great ones. By connecting work to meaning, granting autonomy, and enabling growth, leaders can unlock passionate commitment.

LOOKING AHEAD

Leadership is dynamic, requiring continuous learning and evolution. By applying these principles and staying attuned to emerging conditions, engineering leaders can enable teams to thrive.

In closing, let the insights shared guide you to lead innovative, resilient, results-driven, and passionate teams. May your collective efforts shape a future where technology and humanity prosper together. The principles here equip you for the journey; the rest lies in your hands. Lead wisely, lead boldly, and lead with heart. Onward!

ABOUT THE AUTHOR

Ajay Lakhani is an accomplished engineering leader with over 23 years of experience spanning innovation, complex problem-solving, and spearheading high-performing teams.

As Head of Software Engineering, Ajay has led the successful delivery of large-scale e-commerce platforms. He is skilled in agile methodologies, scalable architecture, and cutting-edge technologies that accelerate time-to-market.

Beyond his technical expertise, Ajay is a passionate advocate for empathetic leadership and nurturing talent. His unique blend of technical vision and business acumen catalyzes excellence in teams.

Ajay is committed to maximizing business impact through technology. His influential leadership has established him as a strategic driver of enterprise digital transformation initiatives.

Through diverse experiences spanning complex engineering initiatives and mentoring talent, Ajay continues to inspire and lead with a lasting impact on the field of software engineering.

Dear Reader,

In "*The Ten Traits of High Performing Engineering Teams*," I delve into the core traits that propel high-performing engineering teams to unparalleled success. These traits, akin to guiding principles, form the bedrock of elite team effectiveness, driving innovation, collaboration, and sustained excellence.

Consider concentrating on one key trait per week, starting with an emphasis on Technical Excellence and concluding with Passionate Engagement. By collectively channeling our attention toward these traits, we can contribute to the elevation of engineering standards and foster a community dedicated to excellence.

With enthusiasm and best wishes,
Ajay Lakhani
https://www.linkedin.com/in/ajaylakhani/

THE TEN TRAITS OF HIGH PERFORMING ENGINEERING TEAMS